Bend in the Stair

Poems

David P. Miller

LILY POETRY REVIEW BOOKS

Copyright © 2021 by David P. Miller

Published by Lily Poetry Review Books
223 Winter Street
Whitman, MA 02382

https://lilypoetryreview.blog/

ISBN: 978-1-7365990-4-4

All rights reserved. Published in the United States by Lily Poetry Review Books. Library of Congress Control Number: 2021936139

Cover design: Martha McCollough

Cover art and author photo: Jane Wiley

Contents

1	Retrieving My Father's Ashes on My Birthday
2	The Story So Far
3	Easter
4	Porches: Wisteria and Its Little Brother
6	Porches: On Chatham Place
8	Quartz, Driftwood
10	This Nectar
12	Mister and Mister and Mister Jazz
14	One Week in May
16	Dinosaur
18	Sunrises With My Father
20	This Could Have Been True
21	His Mouth
23	Keptsakes
24	Like Phantom Limbs
25	One Question I Have About My Ashes
27	Mobius Heart
28	What God Knows
29	Three Hearts
30	Panic
31	Meadowtop: 2006
32	The Days and the Miles
33	The End of That
34	AutoParallel Obit
35	Spring Around Here
36	Our Ideas
38	From a House
40	Little Frogs
41	Porches: The Woodstock Country Inn, Bearsville

42	My Late Father-in-Law's New Project
43	Home Archaeology
45	Add One Father to Earth
50	Leaving the House
52	*Notes*
53	*Acknowledgements*

For my dear Jane
she-out-of-thin-air, karate heroine
siren of newspaper personals, first reader

I needed my mistakes / in their own order / to get me here
- W. S. Merwin, "Wild Oats"

Retrieving My Father's Ashes on My Birthday

It took fewer days for him
to carry me home, lay me in the crib
than for me to carry him home,
place him on a bedroom closet shelf
among the bare clothes hangers.

His wordless gray grit compacted
in the reticent plastic box
weighs about what I did,
pissing, screeching, astounded.

The Story So Far

You made it past the kitchen cockroaches,
some play-acted fumbles at adultery.
Past the DOA M.A. that tripped you
down the garden path to part-time
jobs in slapdash fragments. You made it
past the divorce, then five years
in a gnat-cloud of stillborn lusts.
Past the landlord lineup, a cul-de-sac of bosses.
You even made it past a profession, Professor.

You survived your mother's vacant decay,
sat with your father's final heartbeat.
And you haven't died yet. In the sequel,
you junk their address labels, abort his phone bill,
waste-paper their church programs,
adopt his litter of bookmarks.

The proof you're still alive is your first sighting
of your mother's high school pictures
with her love note in his sock drawer.

Easter

1.
Easter morning with twig-ends bare
as every April, every homely Spring.
Only the most impatient leaf buds
expose themselves, near a month
after equinox. Blossoming muted.
My roots knot to this rhythm.

Our meek city lot's wildlife
persists: squirrels, sparrows, pigeons.
We point and exclaim at a novelty:
a goldfinch at the feeder—its little
body tints the entire yard. Here
the season doesn't know
florist-window eruptions. We settle
with gratitude for each day's
next appearance of unmuzzled color.

2.
This time through, the old blue
above us, we flock as faces
gridded across indoor screens. More faces
arrive, thicken to mosaic.
Shared sunshine fingers each background:
this one's library, that one's kitchen.

On Sunday, we inhale morning walks
through the park, cast side looks
at each other's face masks,
flamboyant or demure.
We not only dress in layers, but
we breathe through them, in the Easter parade
talismans wrapped against our lungs' lockdown.

Porches: Wisteria and Its Little Brother

1.
Rooted thick as a welder's forearm,
our wisteria sprawls green across the chain-link
above the sunken yard.
                In naked months
its skeleton charts a delirious family tree.
When too long untrimmed, it beckons
toward ears of passers-by.
                We find tendrils
ripped away, hurled to the sidewalk.
The fence's bottom edge wrenches out of plumb.

Wisteria has a fetish for the lonely elderly.
Its first caress, with infant finger, seeks
the least crevice beneath the eaves,
the most modest gap in window frame.
                It's a patient, tender romance,
one shingle eased from the next.
Body dismembered plank from desiccated plank.
At last its barked tentacles, grape-cluster
pendant tresses, cuddle-wrap the empty house.
                Glassy-eyed, the house
forgets to fix its face,
forgets to shave or tie its shoes,
sits in the seedy yard, pants around its ankles.

2.
The potted morning glory on the porch,
unstaked this year, thrashes in slow time.
Its feelers grope a silent paramour,
the beach chair I set beside it.
                It's an asymmetric love affair.
Twinings wrap a boa through the frame.
New blossoms push between the webbing.

I might have napped in open air this afternoon,
                found a tentacle at my throat.

Porches: On Chatham Place

In memory of Marjorie Wood Wiley, 1921-2020

A sodden June morning, notebook clumsy on my lap.
Settled on a metal-tube rocking chair,
its arthritic frame inclines backward,

thwacks itself forward. The porch is overhung
enough to sit outside, watch rain plummet thick.
Pen to paper interrupted by a rabbit

at the holly tree, working its jaws,
an engine slurping up the greens. It lopes
the driveway's edge. Infant robins amplify

their starved pleading. A parent bird docks
at the nest, shoves some dangling item
into an offspring maw. We found this nest

outside my wife's childhood bedroom window.
We've returned home to her mother, who remains
indoors, watched over by her aide from bed

to couch to table. Nestlings quiet
as mother or father rockets diagonally
over my corner of the roof. A parent uproots

a worm, drops it on the walk, confirms,
grapples it again. Another unfledged outburst
from beaks gaping famished in the shrub.

Write or watch, exposed and dry, curtained with rain.
That same bird flies again on its same tangent.
The morning steps ahead as the parents

cross off their feed-babies item, then add it back.
Behind the door, we set a day's first coffee.
It gurgles in wait for her mother's waking.

Quartz, Driftwood

1.
This milky quartz stone, each jag
and ledge buffed by the ocean,
answers the light from my eyes
as it settles my hand. Lifted from
the pebble-stippled sand of a Vineyard beach.
Its interior spark ebbed in the wet
but glimmers now as I turn it
beneath the table lamp.

Flat-bottomed wedge mounded
like the old hills we call mountains.
It fits the clutch of my palm,
cools the heart line, the mind line,
the life and fate lines, as they close
around it. Fever's antidote,
it returns no heat. Molten magma
crystallized, permanent ice.

2.
Driftwood bent like a seahorse,
head and tail. Striated, it holds
the living branch's lines of force.
The tree's reach toward the sun
engraved in its double twist.

Three potato-eyed wounds
rise where offspring twigs were
lost. Creases in its bends like skin
set in permanent furrows.
Where it severed from the tree,
the cratered gash is soft, I caress.

It receives my hand's heat.
I stroke this creature, held
against my ear. Its voice, hollow
and low, might be the sigh
of my fingers against grain.

This Nectar

My hand's shadow floats
across the table, projected

from a cloud cover tapestry,
freehand in greys and whites,

light extended from our nearest star.
Our city window almost fully green

with conflagrations at the edges.
Flame flowers saturate the eye,

hold briefly still before the trees
drop their bunting, turn again to rest.

Chill spills from my fingertips.

Here steeps tea from Sri Lanka.
It is beautiful—*shreelanka*, breath

at teeth hushes then melts
amber across the tongue.

My cold body
makes this nectar happen.

The interior kindles
against the skin's anxiety,

its fear to meet the air without
protection, without a tender

carapace of flannel, wool, or down.
The introvert "I" comes forward

with attention still more full
as the mercury contracts, turns shy.

We're all late October.

Mister and Mister and Mister Jazz

Mister and Mister and Mister Jazz hammer it
solid in the café. The fingers of One Mister Jazz
jump and warble. He skitters the tuned-good-enough
low-rise piano flat to a whitewashed wall
of this reprocessed old armory.
Plastic-bound chord charts lean slant
above the keys. Two Mister Jazz battles
the bongos bap bap basement hepcat style.
He skids lyrics from a *real gone* century
over a larynx vibratoed in a somehow tenor.

Snow white skies scat in little pieces.
Fleece-layered families drift down the hall
to the winter farmer's market
under the drill hall ceiling in fuchsia.
Olive oil focaccia, pickled jalapenos,
sour cherry mead, root vegetable spectrum
replace shouldered arms and horse routines.

Three Mister Jazz makes an easy chair
from a random wooden seat. Contemplates
the bridge of his guitar like an elder
retreated from the ridiculous world
to a monk's cave. Two Mister Jazz
bounces his palm off a knee
for all us noshers not snapping fingers,
nodding, shouting *Go Man.*

Mister and Mister and Mister Jazz harvest
a boss green tip jar today. One Mister Jazz's
right hand does the funky roller coaster
as table space wanes and waxes.
Families frown over lacked lunch seats.
Here in this corner a face with frost mustache
scribbles a lime cloth notebook, tops up
with lentil soup. *Do-dad-do-uhm,*
biddly-deh-do dah, bedo-bede-de-um:
Two Mister Jazz twitches hotfoot
across the comfort-food changes.

One Week in May

1. *Airwaves*
On the morning of Harvard radio's "1968 Orgy,"
songs hard-fallen-for or eye-roll-loathed,
Grant Park riot, student strikes snatched from the ether,
my Medicare card grins from the mail.
Don't make it bad, Jude, you're covered.

2. *Productivity*
Outside and squinting to purge yard trash:
overwintered snack wrappers blown from the street.
The tour includes a mouse on its side, intact.
A brass windchime clapper fallen into tree debris.

In the attic, I collapse
cardboard boxes to recycle.
Surprise another box
with great-grandfather's elocution
notebooks—relics of the orator,
Methodist minister who set
a silver dollar on my newborn
tummy. It's a family tale
though nobody living remembers
why. *Ben Hur*'s chariot race,
his blockbuster finale,
sleeps under the lid.

3. *Time Off*
The first iced coffee porch afternoon. Unfold
the director's chair with blue cloth seat, backrest
with my father's name. University colleagues
crafted this present. Who, when, I don't remember.

A skateboarder sails against generally absent traffic:
rainbow bandana wraps her mouth.

A few noises take space between passing cars.
Metal taps from finger pressure
as my pen touches down for fresh attacks.
An airplane: well, someone has a reason to be airborne.

License plates removed from our parents' final cars,
screwed to the porch wall.

4. *Light Waves*
Five souvenir glass pieces in the sun, each fits a hand.
Two pitchers in blue-green and emerald. A sapphire cruet.
A loving cup, a goblet, each one spectrum-saturated
from lemon-yellow base to deep maroon lip.

My mother carried these home from vacations
before there was a 1968 to make a radio orgy out of.
These exact forms, tints and shades:
it's almost not real to me that I have them.
Reunited, I swear, they haven't changed a bit.

Dinosaur

Pterodactyl in bronze. Patina mellows
your wings and belly.

Centered in my palm, your wingtips
press the flesh of thumb and little finger.

Immovable in flight, table-top glider.

How do I deserve you? Remnant memory
of my professor grandfather's study.

When I was a boy, I found you on the desk,
held you, felt myself even more his grandson.

You and the dainty woolly mammoth roughed
of wood. I lifted him, held him to my nose.

Both of you calm oddments of prehistory,
sleepers at night with the genetics journals.

What allowed me to carry you away
when my grandparents departed?

Thirty-four years after the next owners filled
that house with themselves, I drive past.

The front porch is walled, its street face
shut. Something inside must still know me.

The bend in the stair, ascending to the study,
knows who I was. Remembers the extinct creatures.

I took the maple dining chairs and table. I have
the seventeenth-century Bible, the mammoth.

I took you, burnished dinosaur green in my hand.

Sunrises with My Father

1.
My father, settled in a place
where he could walk outdoors all year,
made it his pleasure to help the old folks.
Retired, but barely stepped across
that definite senior-discount line,
he rose each Florida's pre-dawn,
traced on foot the route the "paper boys"
followed to fling the *Sarasota Herald Tribune*
lightly at the ends of driveways.
If these neighbors were the definite elders,
my parents were numbered among the youngers.
He knew the old-old ones by name,
knew which of them needed their news
carried to their porches. Warmth and moisture
soothed his lungs grown rasping
with Massachusetts freeze. Twenty minutes' walk
before the sun burst out with its own baggage
helped to shrink a belly pointlessly enlarged.

I wanted to know something beyond the tourist guides
about this place so easy, soft, and alien.
Some mornings on our visits near the solstice –
those shortened days oddly considered cold –
I'd rise and dress in darkness, shielding my wife's
shut eyes against marauding light,
fumble to the living room to meet him.
Off we'd set, do-gooders at the end of night.
Returned for coffee as bands of red
lifted above the roofs.

2.
Twenty years downstream, my father, a widower,
one of the elder elders, still met the early hours
before I cared to. I'd fumble out to meet him,
his head crooked back on the rose-pink recliner,
shut-eyed after first caffeine. The other
old-olds now fended on their own
for headlines dropped at their driveways' ends.
The younger elder, I stepped into light
for one minuscule good deed, fetched the paper
for his second waking, or his third.

This Could Have Been True

My mother still destroys her Scrabble
opponents, especially her husband
in his fond retreat from the game table.

True, to rise from her chair she depends
on our choreographed hands and a three-toed stick.
But when she commands the board

after dessert, deploys the Q, X, Z tiles,
my father beams like a Klieg light
as he again declines to stand up

against the force of her vocabulary.
His triumph, on this imagined evening
where mind and brain still settle like lovers,

is that she still plays.

His Mouth

1.
"Have you thought about dying?"
This is the pulmonologist's voice
from a room at the other end of the ICU.

I can see a pair of loved ones
just inside that portal, looking toward
their someone in the bed, who may answer

with a quiet word or a look.
We can't tell. My brothers and I
are waiting for the pulmonologist.

We stand outside my father's room
for forty-five minutes, saying nothing,
facing his sedated silence.

When a baby is born in this hospital,
Brahms' "Lullaby" in digital tinkling
murmurs from the intercom.

Two newborns arrive somewhere
as we watch my father's chest
rise and sink. Jagged lines
trace the screen behind him.

2.
His mouth pried open with tubes
for his lungs and gut. He nods
his head at the pulmonologist's
questions: Does he want the tubes
out. Does he know what that means.

We are dismissed for twenty minutes.

We return to his bed
behind drawn goldenrod curtains.
His mouth empty of plastic,
gaped and free, his body unwired.

My brothers tell me they see
movement beneath the light blanket
at his chest. I don't.

Keptsakes

my mother's wheelchair attachment
scraped the driveway's lip
like a dragged tail ornament
chafed our nerves
every time it met the street

my father pressed through back and arms
against handlebars and wife
of fifty-five years

the plywood ramp
carport to front door
angled the rise of the concrete step
spared his strength across the threshold
with his college bride

imagine the half-life of grief
he kept these eight years past need

attachment rusting without its passenger
double prongs cradling no mother's aid
no one fetched a screwdriver

shoe-stained ramp ignored
like an erased welcome mat
no one tossed it for scrap

Like Phantom Limbs

The tiger-maplewood bureau   for example

     after it rolled into the Atlas truck

strapped and swaddled: a piece of inheritance.

     My parents have gone   into photographs.

The bureau's vacant corner   glances

     toward a remnant dining chair:

my mother's post for table-struck dominoes.

     End of the home.   Blanks of removed things.

The dominoes for example   sent to the charity store.

     A mirage of Christmas Eve suppers over the dining table-top.

After Atlas leaves, a son alone can make his body

     fill only one unwanted chair.   At one time.

One Question I Have About My Ashes

Will they still listen? This intact body
pictures itself a relentless listener,
as when remote voices,
nine stories down the well
of a hotel atrium, find the crack
beneath the door. They creep
to the bedside and watch me at night.
This body says, *I can't sleep*,
applies stoppers to its ears,
sets room air low and steady.
This body can set to hibernate
when sound is plain, constant.
But still it hears, hears.

Imagine this chassis gone to motes
running after vibration, the music
of every object. One mote absorbs
what comes just before the chrysalis cracks.
Another hears the broom standing
in place by the pantry. Magazine page
lifted back into air after folding. A sigh
before soil shifts toward the furrow.
An ash picks up a paint chip's unlatch
before it falls from the fanlight
to the porch. What the air says
after the clock hand shifts.
Small sounds no longer obliviated
by solid, bungling ears.

I want my body's scatter to hear
our maple wood chair's two arms
on the porch in summer,
one in sun, the other in shade.
Light and dark songs, each
bonded to its particle of powder.
Twin stars of cinder and sensation.

Mobius Heart

Torqued maple, sliced lean,
formed as a heart. Twisted strips,
fused at the smoothed seams.
I fit it to my palm, embrace one arch
with my thumb. It shelters in my fingers.

Looped wood, two valentine lobes
turned to open as twin chambers.
Bent and joined, a delicate mobius heart.
I follow its calm cross-sections
with my fingertips. Outside becomes
inside without breaking touch.

This heart is made by its empty spaces.
Where the wood is, is its tenderness.
Where the wood isn't,
absence carves its warmth.

Never again an uncarved block. Never
again virgin, unentwined, never
unplaned, unburnished. Two dwellings,
wrapped with a single surface.
Two faces, hers and mine,
without origin or stop.

What God Knows

> *golden shovel, after Jane Hirshfield and Jim Harrison*

Leaves turned, not by breeze in general, but by the
exact wind of a gone moment, now dissolved across dead
evodia twigs and my demurely flaking skin. And do
you consider how much of dust is made of fallen skin? It's not
only that we return to dust. We are dust. Much as we want
our brooms to cleanse the floor, the persistent scatter is us.
Now reconsider each different breeze. When dead

and merged with the empyrean, perhaps with God
we'll know all zephyrs as the one Zephyr that is.
I'm done with fussing over what God knows. Only
let me seize a dustpan of debris, settle myself on
the morning's sweep-up. The celestial part is God's,
I guess, with spent evodia branches left to the side.

Three Hearts

The pelican tips its fish-filled
gut bucket bill to its breast
to press out the last morsels.
The Dalmatian kind rests its blood-
red pouch sagging crimson on its chest.
The old religious made Christ of these.
They saw mother birds pierce
their hearts raw open to feed
their fainting young.

If someone pulls a night blanket's
extra thickness above his heart,
is it that he lacks a piece of quartz
to lull the ache? If at the morning table,
easing eyes on the blue stoneware lamp,
he rests a hand an extra minute
over that place near the breastbone,
is the hand a shield? Armor wrapped
against an average cliff-edge day?
Or a motionless caress, an embrace
of coming strikes, punctures, spills?

The esoteric heart is called *anahata*:
unstruck. It sounds without collision.
Unhurt, it opens bare to all assaults.
Unbeaten say the mystics.
Such image haloes the muscle, certain
in the chest, that beats itself till death.

Panic

Mother, I have your centrifugal illness.
I have the everything at once. As yours,
the spin around to find fear's picture window
shot to shivers. Each full with its own piercings.
Fractals bloomed at the nodes,
and their nodes, and theirs.

That first all-night locked-open eyes
like a doll rigid on its back with a heart
under its own siege. Flung to a tangent,
yes. Classroom teaching crouched on my chest,
flared white eyes braying in the dark.
Each student's blankness looked me
into gnat clouds. Babbling
and zeroed before each gape.

Did you know, my father asked, your mother
never drives herself from home outside a radius
of twenty unlocked minutes? A farther space
snaps the tether. Black drift
outside the capsule. Airless, homeless.

Did you and I ever speak of this
together in one room? I cannot ask you
now, Mother. Could we have slowed
the vertigo down to the earth's rotation?
Held the shapes of each other's specific fright?

Meadowtop: 2006

Mother's arms flow a wide beeline

    spread from her shoulders like hawk wings

        jacket of patchwork and bands   snow toned cobalt blue

            loose sleeves gather mountain sky

Dad's lens mirrors her hues with the Austrian Alps

    a screenplay in layers of mantles behind her

        glasses and smile canted to sunlight

            grass-anchored   heart-choired

after Julie Andrews wheeled on the widescreen

    with her arms splayed like that singing the hills are alive

        picture my mother safeguarded

            this truly happening instant

                how could she not sing for it and spin

The Days and the Miles

from news reports, early 2019

At the border with Mexico, soldiers without
mission sprawl card games across cots. Dismiss
the days with pushups pushed away
from loose panels set in the radiating dirt.
They unfurl one hundred fifty miles
of concertina wire, game scorching footballs,
erect their own toilets. Soldiers deployed
to a will-o'-the-wisp rend MRE bags,
hoping for chicken and noodles
with prize Skittles. Now and again combat
mosquitoes. Drop to heat.

Along the Central Highway, migrants
without weapons stop away from the road
to breastfeed. Wrestle strollers
across the miles, feet again balmed
with iodine. A boy edges the asphalt
cross-legged, his arms propped
sideways to meditate next to his mother
asleep on her clothes bundle. She aims
for Los Angeles where she knows no one
because in my dreams, God told me
that's where he's sending me.

The End of That

golden shovel, after David Byrne/Brian Eno

And
both you
and I may
end before we say
"Bind our shaken hearts to
this whole staring disaster." Shroud yourself,

my
personal God.
Blanch for what
your deep devoted have
torched for your nostrils. I
strip away your shadow. I'm done.

AutoParallel Obit

David P. Miller was born in Cleveland, Ohio on June 21, 1919. He was the son of Bright Army and Lake of Bitterness. He marched for general contracting and taught in the public schools of vine capacity and twig portion. United in marriage to Brave Toy Bear, he wrote two thousand umpire decisions. He passed away on August 26, 1907, aged 75 and 76 (Pennsylvania Volunteers, 107th Regiment).

The attitudes and philosophy of David P. Miller were girdled by the acronym ENCOURAGE: Extension, Nosebreak, Carpentry, Orphism, Undertow, Remission, Avidity, Gloss, Enervation. Although not religious, he is outlasted by children Crooked Nose, Warrior Elf, and One Who Tans Hides; a grandchild, Ewe Herder; and eons of myriads.

What was your experience working with David P. Miller? He was issued in San Jose on October 1, 1946, to the amusement of his family. He relinquished over 22 gallons of blood, he trickled down from Mayflower passengers, he moldered, renowned for his whistling, near Belle Valley at the age of 52. He divulged his belief in a Force for Good.

Dew of the Sea
Dark River
Holder of the Heel
Florida convicted felon (Grand Theft – Firearm)
Best known for *Fast, Cheap & Out of Control* and *Blast-Off Girls*
Attained the rank of Eagle Scout
Would you recommend David P. Miller to others?

David P. Miller does not take on summer interns. He died Tuesday, December 20, 2011, after an extended illness. Do not send requests to be a summer intern. He will not take new graduate students until 2021 or 2022. Want a quote from David P. Miller? Assume the special values that named the fiber of his game: Eventual, Numerary, Chafed, Overwatched, Uvular, Rasorial, Articular, Geotropic, Etceteroid.

There will be no visitation, Tower, Rose, King, or Moon.

Spring Around Here

Spring peeps out from underneath its flannel cover,
groans, rolls back over on its side, chucks the clock
across the room. Spring thinks it's past time we got over
this boresome vernal equinox fixation, sick of our gawk

at straggling, naïve crocuses, forsythia pre-doomed
to shrivel in the wake of premature debuts.
Spring warms in fits, clenches the frigid, loathes perfume.
Lets Winter flirt and tease, hog the gossip and the news.

And screw the sapsuckers. April gives Spring a headache.
Bumblebees arouse its nectar hangover. Maypole dancers
racket and hey-nonny in the hedge: the bed shakes:
Spring calls the cops. They're on parade so no one answers.

Spring tosses back the sheets, puts its peeved face to the window.
Lets fly its yearly whine. Spits out a day of eighty-five degrees,
sneers that maybe now we're satisfied. Stuffs the pillow
underneath the bed. Feet to the floor, flings a final freeze.

Our Ideas

They ask my surrealist wife *Where do you get your ideas?*
as if there were an idea larder
        with odd miscellany:

                One eyeball, an erratic berg
in a Stygian ocean.   A mummified
birdie's body dissolved to branchlets,
slinging a hobo pack, riding a red donut
through an Egyptian waste.

Inventory to stock her worlds
in oil or etching,   glued painted shard wood,
sculpey clay heads,
        pixels numbered   as sand grains in her deserts.

Disgruntled rain droplets in a horde, scowls askew.

She doesn't go anywhere to fetch ideas.
Neither do I.
        Where I did go just now
with my steampunk ballpoint, its sandglass in brass,
was back outside to the blue webbed chair.

                Thought of her and me
before pond sunlight reflected
to leaves' undersides, a hundred or so.
Fractioned mirror over the humble water.

        Locust trees down the other side of our street
shimmer new-yellow all over the car hoods.

All through triangles framed by evodia tree branches.

      Wind in the locusts that side
of the street.   Now breeze quavers here
                          across her face and mine.

               In the middle distance
cottonwood treetops, continuous pixilation.
We unfocus our sight to that glitter,
the pale blue vacancies behind,
               filling and voiding.

From a House

I come from a house built within whiff of breweries now corked,
set at the crotch of a valley whose brook now runs within tubes.
House laughing with tailors, machinists, and trainmen,
brooding with knitters, waiters, furniture movers,
birthday-full of chauffeurs and ironworkers,
vacated by painters, insurance clerks, stagehands.

I come from a house traded and kept by Doyle, Ryan,
    Daley, multiple Murphys,
by and by Zuber and Zwerdling,
doorbelled with Jaime, Rosado, Vassily,
rent-fretted by Baez, Kirikaos, Van Looy,
trudged home and paced overhead by Duggan, Rodriquez, Solsida.
Where home-comers shook off their days of National Shawmut,
    Somerset Hotel, Frank's Lunch, Chimes Brownies,
        wafted their dinners or scooped them from cans.
I come from a house where I came to my she-out-of-thin-air,
    my karate heroine, siren of newspaper personals.

I come from a house of quadruple mortgages,
    when flappers verged on breadlines.
A house whose glass eyed Downy-Flake Donuts,
    Hauschildt Distilled Spirits, Roxbury Mattress.
    (A pox after that of emptying lots.)
I come from a house bought out from under city-condemning,
    its price nailed to the porch,
    upper third hollowed of walls and plumbing.
A house with decades of martial art foot landings,
    massaged hard into blonde polish.
That held itself free from sparks from the torched mattress
    née stringed instrument factory.
    (The lot's palimpsest soil turned up tubes of catgut.)

I come from a house with bedroom carpeted floor to ceiling,
    a flipped shower where Cold is code word for Hot.
A house where four now go out and come back, with a homebody mouse.
    (Surprised in the kitchen, it dives down a burner.)
A house rooted on thickness of puddingstone.
A house that shares the water of earth in its basement.
A house that stirs in its sleep with the passage of night trains.

Little Frogs

April thirteen after dark. Long Island
spring peepers have called for hours.
Whistle bubbles decibeled like motorcycles
from little throats hidden in leaf mold.

This does not cohabit well with flux
from my laptop's mouth open on the dining table,
or death threats spat against the congresswoman
in her hijab. Not well with Vermonters' homes

washed away into eroding ravines
while the lone podcast comment grabs
his nethers, barks *it's weather, suck it up.*

Nickel-sized hoppers sing their mating madrigals
pondside. This suburb of trees and undulation
allows them transient vernal pools.

Otherwise the runoff is loyal: floods
refuse us so far. Water slips down-street
past the mailbox with its cast iron post-boy.
The lawns take it up, mostly.

My father-in-law's old woodlot sinks
into its decades' moist time: log splits
that will never meet a hearth.

Inherited luck shelters in this dim room:
twin pools of table lamplight inside,
tiny peepers' massed vibrations outside.

I banish cookie-cuttered pundits, their
writhing mouths, from all my screens.
I can pull shades tight to the sills
and not see darkness either.

Porches: The Woodstock Country Inn, Bearsville

Tara annihilates mugwort stalks with vinegar spray.
They brown from the base upwards. Vinegar wind
perfuses up to me on the porch. Something's pickled.
Swallowtails, lightly exiled, flee abutting butterfly bushes.

A speck-size green spider hesitates to mount the edge
of my notebook. The day heads toward ninety. Laundry
lifts in the light breeze like Wilbur's angels. Pillowcases, bedsheets

from the sleep of the Danish couple who shared Tara's pancakes
across the table this morning. She works for the diplomatic service,
he the Ministry of Defense. Denmark shovels two-thirds less GDP
to defense than we do. We are not three times happier than Denmark.

The laundry basket's white, the picnic table beneath the flowing maple
white. White wicker chairs decay genteel on our ivory and white
overlook. We have taken the White Room, everything like that,
not sparing throw rugs. David Bowie rented this house ten summers.

Yesterday, a coyote at the border of grass and woods, beyond the gravel
car park. He allowed eye contact before shying off to the trees.
Beyond butterfly bushes and perishing mugwort the hill falls
to an entire high garden of deciduous and evergreen, wedges of Catskills.

Sheets flap. A swallow on a dead branch flicks its tail.
A bee makes itself heard on its course straight past my ear.
I'm thinking of a man who had been but was not the Thin White Duke,

had been but was no longer Ziggy Stardust, at this porch glass table.
The coyote wails from the hills beside him. It fell to Earth,
my first "Life on Mars," insisted from my high school FM
in a plastic radio box, hippie station faint from a distant city.

My Late Father-in-Law's New Project

In memory of Joseph Norris Wiley, 1919-2012

In his hospice room, Joe took an exit alone.
But our electrical engineer,
relentless inventor, never lacks
a fresh direction, even now in a place
beyond language. He rewires the forest
though we can't unearth the apparatus.
It's all his workshop: like the stream
you hear, wait, isn't that sound
a bit too much elsewhere?
The same impending babble, augmented
to widen the radius of hiker's delight.

We'll never guess his algorithm
for autumn. Each leaf fully chromatic,
not one dull, not remnant-green after time,
but the circuits can't be found.
The data, desirably obscure.

These woods — still his workbenches,
his inventor's broad basement.
He experiments with new barks,
shuffles fungal forms,
scraps the dead ends,
redrafts and gets out of the way.

Home Archaeology

      Knotted-hemp-rope belt from teendom
without a fastener. Whose waist
would that clasp? Could have clasped?
Its short length, implausible.

      The high school diploma, proof
against future social media exposés
wielded to take down my whole career
ex post facto.

      Six pairs of glasses,
half of them tape-wrapped at the joints.

      Beltless buckles: Celtic knot,
Indian head nickel, Alice pushed through
her mantel mirror's backside.

      God help us, my doggerel high school song lyrics.

Death cleaning, even through the underwear drawer, never too early.

      Father's wedding ring fleetingly lost.
The hospital morgue didn't have it, survived
clothes bag didn't hold it. It wasn't on his hand
at last. He laid it in the scatter of her remnant jewelry,
then implored an ambulance. Reappeared
as we harrowed his bedroom.

      At least seven of my brown-haired IDs.
Brass alumni association stickpin.
      Polished quartz cufflinks set in silver.
When did I ever wear cufflinks?

Letter composed on *Yellow Submarine*
stationery, *to:* address menaced by the Flying Glove,
to a girl I liked about another girl I loved and oh
my damaged young heart. Never
sent, still sealed, shuttled from drawer
to drawer damn near fifty years.

His wallet with two cards for the final
defibrillator. Driver's license, one drooped eyelid
confirmed by the camera. Same lid as mine.

The license itself alive yet
for four years, nine months, eighteen days.

Add One Father to Earth

1.
Shelved where his shoes had been,
his unrested ashes waited in a black lidded box
in stout plastic held close in his vacant clothes closet
above the hamper where I threw the garments
he wore to ride in his final ambulance.

After sixteen weeks I carried them through the Florida city.
At the airport they were scanned with a smile for explosives.

In Massachusetts his ashes rode with us
past a weed-ridden car dealership.
No one but me remembers
the small-town lunch spot in that place. We scavenged
our first nothing-open-Sunday sandwiches there.
One last trip past that obliterated memory

on the way to the church of dwindling
recollections, church for thirty years before
my parents' migration toward lawn egrets and ditches
for stormwater. Returned back from Paradise
to the church where my father troweled
my mother's remains seven years before.

Where we then committed his. So much human grit.
Seventeen people stooped to the earth.
Now it settles in earth, uncoffined,
unmarked, fluid as matter through matter.

A remnant preserved for my desk
in a modest marble urn, before me
on a blue October with its stubborn
city greenness of trees.

2.
He lifted his free right arm
from beneath his hospital blanket.
Forced speechless by the apparatus
propelling his lungs, he opened his hand
toward us. His fingers curved one by one
in a cascade against his palm, little finger
rippling toward index finger.
He did this three times. We saw it,
the gentle opening and graceful closing
of his grip. We didn't understand.

He then spread his palm to face us, moved it
side to side in-towards and out-away from him.
This we understood, because as children
we learned to wave when it was time
to go from someone.

But first, he spread and curled his fingers
to grasp no one's offered hand.
                              I saw this and I blanked.
When I first held
the density of his remains, I realized
what he had asked of us.
I knew it only then.

3.
Sixteen weeks' stillness on his closet shelf,
the closet in service to their bedroom.
Waking one morning, he told my mother he couldn't
do it anymore, could not, could no longer
lift her, walk her, feed her.
A nursing home opened to her before sundown.

Sixteen weeks sacked
in resolute plastic necked by a dog tag
in a snap-brim box in a floral yellow shopping bag
of sympathy.

4.
Famished family lost without lunch
in our new little town. Sunday noon
in 1963, Lord's-Day-we're-closed. Nothing
in the cupboard. The movers left us.
We'd hauled our trek from corn country Indiana
to tobacco shed Massachusetts,
the best asparagus earth on earth.
The Gronostalski onion truck, prodigious
Polish name festooned wide in paint
fading even then. Stan the Vegetable Man
whose beacon sign blazoned a man
figured, yes, of vegetables.
These decaying stalwarts still held the roadside
fifty years later, wayposts for homecomers.
But brand new then, still lunchless,
we roamed Route 9 in the red Rambler,
three cranky boys, two disoriented parents.
Who could tell how this little lunch place arose
like a vision, the Spruce Hill Restaurant,
a Brigadoon of sandwiches.
That eatery of the first day of the rest of our lives.

At some erased moment between then and now
the slope-roofed lunch box poked its sides out,
glassed its front to sell autos. Failed quickly.
There are its stubborn barren windows, shameless stains,
opportunist weeds: souvenir I remember and reject.
Something of my father goes for his final ride

past our first meal. And I want to challenge
someone: find the strength to take
this forsaken hulk, render it to atoms, lay it down.

5.
Grit the color of faint afterfeathers
in an equable porcelain bowl
set near dug-out earth.
A car radio edges the church sidewalk
beyond the garden. The thought
of entertainment by subwoofer serenade
frets me. And there is a lot of ash.

Four sons, two wives, two girlfriends, grandson,
each settles a ceremonial scoopful
in the empty space. Still there is much ash.

I call to the witnesses, make impromptu
community event of this. Four cousins,
two husbands, put their hands to the work.
Sister-in-law's father and stepmother take it up.
Each in stillness with their minds arcing
toward the trowel, its mass.

Christ, there is so much ash left.

I squat, take the bowl at the lip,
empty his persisting remains
directly into the gape
like cups of flour into a mixing bowl.
I don't want that image.
But maybe it is that image.
Add one father to earth.
Cover and let stand overnight.
Let stand permanently.

6.
Let stand permanently,
that tablespoon-worth of him saved
before passage through the airport,
before passing the first-lunch ruin,
before the memorial garden.
Saved for a desktop urn, veined
in lightning bolts of rust-red with patches
of near-white like elderly skin.
Marble monument cool
against my palm, fingers wrap
like tendrils around the jar.
Fragment or fractal of the gravestone
he refused with adamance.
He would not be left as a site
of pilgrimage, a chiseled name
filled over time with lichen, a site
of contrite visits, first rare, then none.
Instead, he is at home with me
while my home persists,
before me in the shifting
late October sun. I close my eyes
against the waxing daylight,
open them upon his urn again
in the temporary darkness.

Leaving the House

In your final hour in the final place

where your parents chose to live,

the things your family asked for trucked to Massachusetts,

ready to quit a cordial elder neighborhood

for which you had no further earthly use,

you embraced the house.

Moved from room to room. Arms stretched wide,

you pressed against the walls, kissed them.

Walked out, down the wheelchair ramp,

left house keys for the realtor to find,

shut yourself inside the rental car,

and drove away from the end.

Notes

Many of these poems are in memory of Dorothy M. Miller (1934-2011) and Melton M. Miller, Jr. (1933-2018).

"What God Knows": the source poems for this "golden shovel" are Jane Hirshfield's "The Dead Do Not Want Us Dead" and Jim Harrison's "Poem of War."

"The End of That": "golden shovel" after a line from the Talking Heads song "Once in a Lifetime."

Acknowledgments

My thanks to the publications in which the following poems first appeared (many in earlier versions):

Constellations: "One Question I Have About My Ashes," "Panic"
Denver Quarterly: "Like Phantom Limbs"
Foliate Oak: "This Could Have Been True"
Hawaii Pacific Review: "Retrieving My Father's Ashes on My Birthday"
Lily Poetry Review: "What God Knows"
Meat for Tea: "His Mouth"
Muddy River Poetry Review: "Dinosaur"
New England Poetry Club Prize-Winners' Anthology: "Add One Father to Earth"
Nixes Mate Review: "From a House"
Peacock Journal: "Quartz, Driftwood"
Silkworm: "The Story So Far"
What Rough Beast: "The End of That"

"Add One Father to Earth" was awarded an honorable mention, by judge Robert Pinsky, for the New England Poetry Club's 2019 Samuel Washington Allen Prize competition.

The majority of these poems have benefitted greatly from discussion in Tom Daley's night workshop at the Boston Center for Adult Education; Kevin McLellan's workshop in Cambridge, Massachusetts; and the Boston Poetry Workshop led by Zachary Bos. I am grateful to Shana Hill for her conscientious effort on behalf of my work. Special thanks go to Eileen Cleary for her support of this project, and to Lisa Sullivan, my editor, for her close and insightful readings.

ABOUT THE AUTHOR

David P. Miller's collection, *Sprawled Asleep,* was published by Nixes Mate Books in 2019. His chapbook, *The Afterimages,* was published by Červená Barva Press in 2014. With a background in experimental theater and performance before turning to poetry, David was a member of the multidisciplinary Mobius Artists Group of Boston for 25 years. He was a librarian at Curry College in Massachusetts, from which he retired in June 2018. He and his wife, the visual artist Jane Wiley, live in the Jamaica Plain neighborhood of Boston.

www.ingramcontent.com/pod-product-compliance
Lightning Source LLC
Chambersburg PA
CBHW020915080526
44589CB00011B/603